OUR FAVORITE BRANDS

DISNEY

By Emma Huddleston

Kaleidoscope
Minneapolis, MN

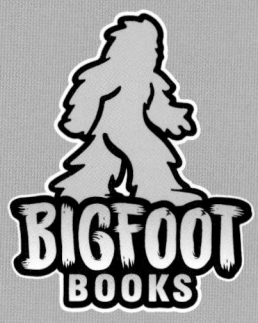

The Quest for Discovery Never Ends

This edition is co-published by agreement between Kaleidoscope and World Book, Inc.

Kaleidoscope Publishing, Inc.
6012 Blue Circle Drive
Minnetonka, MN 55343 U.S.A.

World Book, Inc.
180 North LaSalle St., Suite 900
Chicago IL 60601 U.S.A.

All rights reserved. No part of this book may be reproduced in any form without written permission from the publishers.

Kaleidoscope ISBNs
978-1-64519-012-7 (library bound)
978-1-64494-177-5 (paperback)
978-1-64519-112-4 (ebook)

World Book ISBN
978-0-7166-4312-8 (library bound)

Library of Congress Control Number
2019939226

Text copyright ©2020 by Kaleidoscope Publishing, Inc. All-Star Sports, Bigfoot Books, and associated logos are trademarks and/or registered trademarks of Kaleidoscope Publishing, Inc.

Printed in the United States of America.

FIND ME IF YOU CAN!

Bigfoot lurks within one of the images in this book. It's up to you to find him!

TABLE OF CONTENTS

Chapter 1: The Most Magical Place on Earth 4

Chapter 2: The Disney Story 10

Chapter 3: Movies and Beyond 16

Chapter 4: Disney Around the World 22

Beyond the Book 28
Research Ninja 29
Further Resources 30
Glossary 31
Index 32
Photo Credits 32
About the Author 32

CHAPTER 1

Walt Disney World in Orlando, Florida, is crowded with millions of visitors each year.

The Most Magical Place on Earth

May's heart pounded. She handed her ticket to the smiling worker. He scanned it and gave it back. Her mother grabbed her hand. May took her little brother Oscar's hand. Together, they walked into the most magical place on earth. They were at the Magic Kingdom at Walt Disney World.

Colorful shops lined the street. Crowds of people walked around. May turned her head from side to side. She saw stuffed animals in a shop window. Shelves of candy were in another. The smell of popcorn was in the air. May couldn't believe her eyes. Cinderella Castle stood in the middle of the park.

May felt like a princess. She pulled on her mother's hand. She wanted to see Cinderella. Maybe Mickey and Minnie would walk by. She hoped to see all her favorite Disney characters.

Disney World has four main parks. May's favorite was Magic Kingdom. Oscar liked Disney's Animal Kingdom. It has a zoo. Monkeys and birds live there. There's a huge tree in the middle. Oscar loved seeing the tigers. One yawned. May and Oscar saw all of his teeth. May liked the elephants. They reminded her of Dumbo.

DISNEY MAGIC

Walt Disney dreamed of bringing his movies and characters to life. He created theme parks. Disneyland opened in California in 1955. Then Disney World opened in Florida in 1971. People from all over the world visited. More than fifty million people visit Disney World each year.

At Disney theme parks around the world, visitors can enjoy thrilling Disney-themed rides.

They watched fireworks at the end of the day. May and Oscar got **souvenirs**. May got a toy Stitch from *Lilo & Stitch*. Oscar got a Lightning McQueen T-shirt. They would never forget their trip to Disney World.

FUN FACT
There are six Disney resorts around the world.

Disney's Animal Kingdom is home to many beautiful animals.

CHAPTER 2

The Disney Story

Walt Disney loved to draw. He took art classes in school. He wanted to be a cartoonist. Disney created his first **animated** films in 1920. He was nineteen years old. He called them Laugh-O-Grams. They were only a few minutes long. The local theater played them between movies. People thought they were clever. He made a little money from them.

But Disney didn't have much. He slept in his office in Kansas City, Missouri. Mice crawled on the floor at night. They nibbled on food crumbs. One mouse was brave. It became Disney's friend. He let it live in his desk drawer. The mouse crawled on Disney's paper as he drew.

Disney moved to California in 1923. He wanted to make movies. The mouse from his old office inspired him. He created the character Mickey Mouse. He drew a big smile on Mickey's face. Disney's pen scratched the paper as he colored. He drew big, round ears on Mickey's head. Disney made his first Mickey Mouse film in 1928. It was a black-and-white **comedy**. It was called *Steamboat Willie.* It was seven minutes long.

Walt Disney began making animated films when he was nineteen years old.

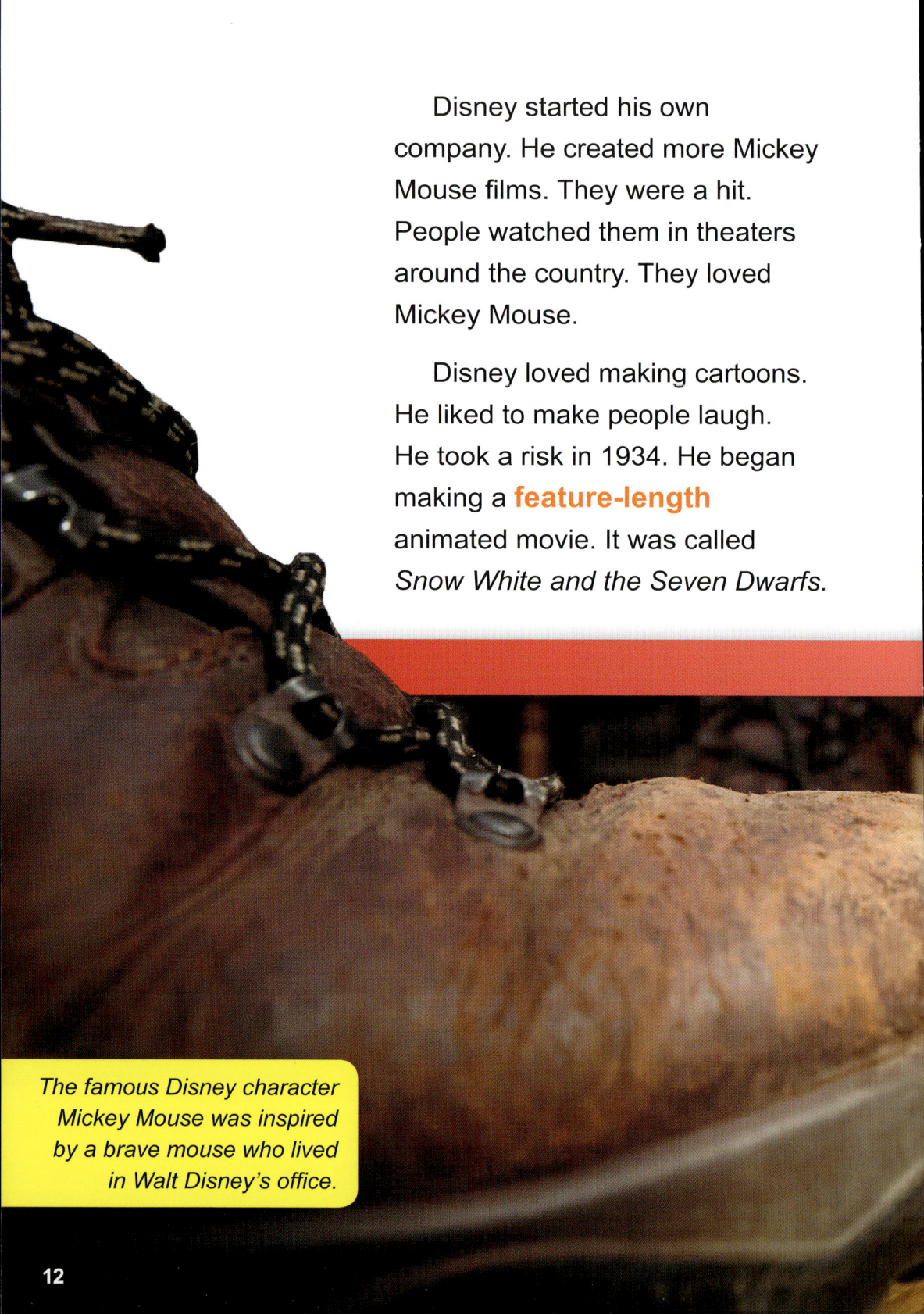

Disney started his own company. He created more Mickey Mouse films. They were a hit. People watched them in theaters around the country. They loved Mickey Mouse.

Disney loved making cartoons. He liked to make people laugh. He took a risk in 1934. He began making a **feature-length** animated movie. It was called *Snow White and the Seven Dwarfs.*

The famous Disney character Mickey Mouse was inspired by a brave mouse who lived in Walt Disney's office.

It was much longer than any other cartoon he had made. It was one hour and twenty-three minutes. He didn't know if it would be successful.

It was finished in 1937. People loved it. Each dwarf was unique. The evil queen was cruel. People wanted to see how the story ended.

Snow White was the first of many Disney films. Disney kept making animated movies. He made *Bambi* and *Cinderella.* Then, he started making **live-action** films and TV shows. Disney entertained families and people of all ages.

FUN FACT
Mickey Mouse was originally named Mortimer Mouse.

DISNEY TIMELINE

1983 Disney Channel begins airing television shows.

1937 *Snow White and the Seven Dwarfs* premieres.

1950 *Cinderella*

Disney's first live-action film, *Treasure Island*, is released.

1965 Disney receives five Academy Awards for *Mary Poppins*.

1920 Walt Disney creates the first Laugh-O-Gram animated film.

1959 *Sleeping Beauty*

1971 Walt Disney World in Florida has its grand opening.

1920 1930 1940 1950 1960 1970 1980

1942 *Bambi*

1970 *The Aristocats*

1928 *Steamboat Willie* is released.

1961 *One Hundred and One Dalmatians*

1955 Disneyland in Anaheim, California, has its grand opening.

Lady and the Tramp

1977 *The Many Adventures of Winnie the Pooh*

1989
The Little Mermaid

1992
Aladdin

1991
Beauty and the Beast

1994
The Lion King

1995
Pocahontas

1997
Hercules

1998
Mulan

1999
Tarzan

2000
The Emperor's New Groove

2002
Lilo & Stitch

2006
Disney purchases Pixar.

2009
Disney purchases Marvel Entertainment.

2009
The Princess and the Frog

2010
Tangled

2012
Wreck-It Ralph

Disney purchases Lucasfilm, the company behind *Star Wars*.

2013
Frozen

2014
Big Hero 6

2015
Disney begins making live-action remakes of some of their original animated films. These include *Cinderella*, *Beauty and the Beast*, and *Aladdin*.

2016
Zootopia

Moana

1990   1995   2000   2005   2010   2015   2020

15

CHAPTER 3

Movies and Beyond

Disney reaches people in many ways. Miguel's dad turns up the volume in the car. Radio Disney plays. Miguel's little sister sings along to a song from *Frozen*. She yells, "Let it go! Let it go!" She throws her hand in the air. His sister also loves Disney Channel. She likes to watch *Andi Mack* after school.

Disney Channel airs shows like Andi Mack *and* Tangled: The Series *for young viewers.*

FUN FACT
Elsa from *Frozen* was originally going to be the movie's villain.

The superhero movie *Black Panther* was made by Disney and Marvel Studios.

Miguel is excited. His family is going to the movie theater. The last movie they saw was *Black Panther*. Miguel loved it. *Black Panther* was made by Disney and Marvel. Those companies joined in 2009. Today, his family is going to see *Incredibles 2.* Disney and Pixar made this one together. Disney bought Pixar in 2006.

At the movie, Miguel's dad spills popcorn on the floor. A loud fight scene made him jump. Miguel and his sister giggle. Miguel thinks Violet is the best. He wants to make force fields with his mind.

Disney Stores sell toys, clothes, games, and other products featuring popular Disney characters.

Bella walks into the Disney Store at the mall. She is looking for a *Brave* shirt. Bella wants to be an archer like Princess Merida. She learned archery in gym class last year. She walks past stuffed animals and princess dolls.

FUN FACT
There are more than 200 Disney Stores worldwide.

She sees movies and video games. There are books about all her favorite characters. She finds the clothes. The T-shirt shows Merida in the woods. She holds her bow and arrow. Bella can't wait to show her friends at school.

CHAPTER 4

Disney Around the World

In 1942, Walt Disney received an award. He wiped tears from his eyes. The award is given to talented **producers**. It is for people who change the film industry. Walt Disney was honored.

Disney films have received many awards. The Academy Awards is an awards ceremony for movies. They give out Oscars. Many Disney films have been **nominated** for Oscars. Disney won the Best Animated Feature Film award in 2018. It's won it almost every year since 2006.

The team behind Big Hero 6 *celebrated winning the Oscar for Best Animated Feature Film in 2015.*

TOP 15 ANIMATED DISNEY MOVIES
by Box Office Sales

Incredibles 2	$606.8 million
Finding Dory	$486.3 million
The Lion King	$422.8 million
Toy Story 3	$415.0 million
Frozen	$400.7 million
Finding Nemo	$380.8 million
Inside Out	$356.5 million
Zootopia	$341.3 million
Up	$293.0 million
Monsters, Inc.	$289.9 million
Monsters University	$268.5 million
The Incredibles	$261.4 million
Moana	$248.8 million
Toy Story 2	$245.9 million
Cars	$244.1 million

Amura watched *Moana*. It was playing in Tahitian, her native language. She couldn't believe it. The movie had bright colors. It had upbeat, catchy songs. Moana was independent. She went on a risky journey to save her community.

In French Polynesia, thousands of people attended public screenings of the Tahitian version of Moana *in 2017.*

Disney translates its movies into more than forty languages. The most common ones are French, German, and Spanish. *Moana* was the first Disney movie **dubbed** in Tahitian.

FUN FACT
Mickey Mouse was the first animated character to get a star on the Hollywood Walk of Fame.

Thanks to Disney and the Make-A-Wish Foundation, children around the world have their wishes to visit Disney theme parks come true.

Disney makes a difference in more than just movies. Mila went to Disneyland Paris in France. She met Mickey Mouse. She gave him a hug. His soft fur brushed her cheek. Her family took a picture. They were celebrating Mila. She beat cancer. Mila had always wanted to go to Disneyland. The Make-A-Wish Foundation and Disney made it happen. They work together to grant wishes for very sick kids. They've made more than 130,000 wishes come true.

Disney keeps growing. It offers new movies, shows, and toys. Kids like May and Mila love Disney's theme parks. They see their favorite characters come to life. Around the world, Disney makes people smile.

DISNEY AND NATURE

The Disney Conservation Fund wants to save animals. It works with at-risk species. It helps monkeys, sea turtles, tigers, and more. It also wants to protect Earth. It supports projects that help the environment. The Disney Conservation Fund has given more than $75 million to help wildlife.

BEYOND THE BOOK

After reading the book, it's time to think about what you learned. Try the following exercises to jumpstart your ideas.

THINK

THAT'S NEWS TO ME. *Moana* was the first Disney movie translated into Tahitian. Where could you find information about the first screenings of the Tahitian version of *Moana*? How could those sources fill in more detail about the event?

CREATE

PRIMARY SOURCES. A primary source is an original document or object. It provides firsthand information about a person or event. Interviews, photographs, and diary entries are all examples of primary sources. Create a list of primary sources you might be able to find about Disney.

SHARE

SUM IT UP. Write a paragraph summarizing the important points from the whole book. Don't just copy the book. Use your own words to tell the story of Disney. Then, share the paragraph with a classmate. Does your classmate have any feedback on the summary or additional questions about Disney?

GROW

DRAWING CONNECTIONS. Create a diagram that shows and explains the connections between Disney and animation. How does learning about animation help you better understand Disney?

RESEARCH NINJA

Visit *www.ninjaresearcher.com/0127* to learn how to take your research skills and book report writing to the next level!

RESEARCH

DIGITAL LITERACY TOOLS

SEARCH LIKE A PRO
Learn about how to use search engines to find useful websites.

FACT OR FAKE?
Discover how you can tell a trusted website from an untrustworthy resource.

TEXT DETECTIVE
Explore how to zero in on the information you need most.

SHOW YOUR WORK
Research responsibly— learn how to cite sources.

WRITE

GET TO THE POINT
Learn how to express your main ideas.

PLAN OF ATTACK
Learn prewriting exercises and create an outline.

DOWNLOADABLE REPORT FORMS

Further Resources

BOOKS

Johnson, Mindy. *Pencils, Pens & Brushes: A Great Girls' Guide to Disney Animation.* Disney Press, 2019.

Kramer, Barbara. *Walt Disney.* National Geographic, 2017.

Suen, Anastasia. *Video Animation and Photography.* Rourke Educational Media, 2017.

WEBSITES

FACTSURFER

Factsurfer.com gives you a safe, fun way to find more information.

1. Go to www.factsurfer.com.
2. Enter "Disney" into the search box and click 🔍.
3. Select your book cover to see a list of related websites.

Glossary

animated: An animated film is made using many drawings shown back-to-back so they seem to move. Disney's first Mickey Mouse movie was an animated film called *Steamboat Willie.*

comedy: A comedy is a movie that is meant to make people laugh. *Toy Story* is an example of a comedy.

dubbed: A movie is dubbed when a version is recorded in another language. Disney dubbed *Moana* into another language.

feature-length: Some award groups define a feature-length film as a movie that is more than forty minutes long, but feature films usually last anywhere from ninety minutes to two hours. Disney made four feature-length films between 1940 and 1942.

live-action: A live-action film features real people acting, rather than animated characters. Disney's first live-action film was called *Treasure Island.*

nominated: Something is nominated when it is suggested or recommended for an award or other honor. Disney movies are nominated for awards almost every year.

producers: Producers are in charge of making a movie or paying for it to be made. Walt Disney is one of the most famous film producers in history.

souvenirs: Souvenirs are toys or objects that remind a person of an experience, especially a vacation. Many Disney World and Disneyland souvenirs are based on characters from Disney movies.

Index

awards, 14, 22

box office sales, 23

Disney, Walt, 6, 10, 12–13, 14, 22

Disney Channel, 14, 16

Disney Conservation Fund, 27

Disney Stores, 20–21

Disneyland California, 6, 14

Disneyland Paris, 27

live-action films, 13, 14–15

Make-A-Wish, 27

Marvel, 15, 19

Mickey Mouse, 6, 10, 12, 13, 25

Moana, 15, 23, 24–25

Pixar, 15, 19

Snow White and the Seven Dwarfs, 12–13, 14

Steamboat Willie, 10, 14

timeline, 14–15

translation, 24–25

Walt Disney World, 5–6, 8, 14

PHOTO CREDITS

The images in this book are reproduced through the courtesy of: WendyOlsenPhotography/iStockphoto, front cover (castle); s_bukley/Shutterstock Images, front cover (Mickey Mouse); dean bertoncelj/Shutterstock Images, front cover (princesses); kamui29/Shutterstock Images, pp. 3, 15 (bottom left); John Raoux/AP Images, pp. 4–5; cholprapha/iStockphoto, pp. 6–7; Mercury Green/Shutterstock Images, p. 8; Humble 4 Real Photos/Shutterstock Images, pp. 8–9; Bettmann/Getty Images, pp. 10–11; DamianKuzdak/iStockphoto, pp. 12–13; Air Elegant/Shutterstock Images, p. 13; TK Kurikawa/Shutterstock Images, p. 14 (top); TkKurikawa/iStockphoto, 14 (bottom left); Nicescene/Shutterstock Images, pp. 14 (bottom right), 30; Red Line Editorial, p. 23 (chart); Bruno Ismael Silva Alves/Shutterstock Images, p. 15 (top); Michael Gordon/Shutterstock Images, p. 15 (bottom right); Kathy Hutchins/Shutterstock Images, pp. 16–17; Amawasri Pakdara/Shutterstock Images, p. 17; Sarunyu L/Shutterstock Images, pp. 18–19; canbedone/Shutterstock Images, pp. 20–21; Jordan Strauss/Invision/AP Images, p. 22; M. Unal Ozmen/Shutterstock Images, p. 23 (popcorn); Gregory Boissy/AFP/Getty Images, pp. 24–25; MarKord/iStockphoto, p. 26.

ABOUT THE AUTHOR

Emma Huddleston has written books about science, sports, animals, and more. When she isn't writing, she enjoys reading and swing dancing. She lives in the Twin Cities with her husband.